THE BEGINNERS GUIDE TO
SHOTOKAN KARATE

GICHIN FUNAKOSHI
The father of modern day karate, who was a scholar of the Chinese classics as well as a karate master, was born in Shuri, Okinawa Prefecture, in 1868 and died in Tokyo in 1957.

The Beginners Guide

SHOTOKAN
KARATE

by
John van Weenen
5th Dan

Chief Instructor:
Traditional Association of Shotokan Karate

Paul Hooley and Associates
BEDFORD

First published November 1983
First Reprint April 1984
Second Reprint October 1985
Third Reprint August 1986
Fourth Reprint May 1987
Fifth Reprint January 1988
Sixth Reprint April 1989

ISBN NO 0 905095 01 4

Published by Paul Hooley and Associates, 29 Elstow Road, Kempston, Bedford.
Printed by Newnorth-Burt Limited, Newnorth House, College Street, Kempston, Bedford.

I dedicate this book to my wife Jane

CONTENTS

PREFACE

The reasons that led me to write this book are many, however, the over-riding and deciding factor was the beginner's need for an elementary instruction manual that covered the three basic aspects of Karate training, written by a Westerner for Westerners.

The majority of books on the market today have been written by Japanese, and quite rightly so, for in my opinion, they are better qualified to write and teach Karate-Do than any other people. Having said that, in my experience over the last 20 years, many books have tended to be a little overpowering for the average beginner, consequently, he learns very little from them.

I hope "The Beginner's Guide to Shotokan Karate" will rectify this. It is intended as a manual to assist club training and to enable the beginner to follow the basic fundamentals that he has been taught by his own teacher. Of course technique will differ from instructor to instructor, each having his own "Body System" but by and large Shotokan is universal in its basic concepts, and the reader should bear this in mind when comparing techniques.

As a traditionalist, I feel some measure of responsibility in the continuance of Karate-Do as a way of life, not merely as a sport, for I feel if the art has survived since the Sixth Century, it *must* be good and have a great deal to offer, otherwise it would have disappeared a long long time ago.

May I take this opportunity of thanking Mr Trevor Yorke who so painstakingly took the many photographs and Mr Paul Hooley my Printer and Publisher without whose help this book would not have been possible.

John van Weenen
November 1983

A BEGINNERS VIEW

I came to Karate by chance. Oh I had from time to time observed groups of exponents in various positions of self-defence, and my son was a keen participant, but it never occurred to me that here was an activity with which I would become involved, let alone enthralled by.

As a lapsed sportsman of approaching middle years, it was the organised keep fit that first attracted me – the twenty minute warm-up period that, under the guidance of trained experts, systematically and scientifically stretched and toned up all the muscles and sinews of the body.

I soon discovered, almost without realising the fact, that I had entered into the spirit of Karate, and having come to terms with the early movements, I became aware of a re-awakening of a forgotten boyhood emotion – anticipation. As I looked forward to each new lesson, I would practice at home in front of the bathroom mirror.

It was at this stage, however, that I became a little frustrated. My problems, in common with others no doubt, were two-fold. Firstly in remembering the sequence of previously taught movements, and secondly, being a less than gifted linguist, in grasping the Japanese commands and terminology. As a consequence I was forever Gyaku-tzuki-ing when I should have been Mae-geri-ing.

My disappointment was in being unable to find any suitable publication aimed at the beginner, that supplemented the lessons of the Dojo, was written in basic Western terms, explained simply and pictorially the movements, and served as quick, yet comprehensive reference guide.

Life, however, is very much about being in the right place at the right time. For me to have come to the sport under the guidance of Sensei van Weenen was indeed a stroke of good fortune, and when he asked me to assist him in producing such a book, aimed primarily for the benefit of the beginner, I was naturally delighted.

My observation is that Karate brings untold benefits to its fortunate exponents – confidence, physical fitness, self-defence, and so much more. By its very teachings it instills the virtues of honour and consideration, encouraging always a greater awareness of one's fellow creatures, and a genuine desire to leave only pleasant and fond memories as one journey's along "The Way".

If this book assists in achieving any of these objectives it will have provided a worthwhile service to the individual, and have been of benefit to Karate Do.

Paul Hooley

Left: In the Dojo – Sensei and student, author and publisher

FOREWORD

John van Weenen is well suited to author this book on Shotokan
Karate, having trained for twenty years with the great names of the
style. John is one of the few westerners who can appreciate that there
is more to Karate than the purely physical. The very use he makes of the
word "Traditional" in the title of his own association confirms that he is
devoted to the deeper aspects of this fascinating art. It is so very
important, when learning Karate, to understand that it is more than just
an impressive physical system; it is a deep philosophy and a unique
expression of the Japanese warrior spirit. To teach the techniques
without the underlying meaning and significance is only to graze the
surface.
I well remember my teachers patiently explaining the importance of
attitude to training; the need to train and constantly return to basics. It
is only by constantly practising the basic techniques of Karate that the
student can learn to react instinctively. The proper practice of Karate –
as described in John's excellent book – leaves the mind calm and
relaxed. It becomes cleared of the clutter of pre-conceptions and
"when to do what". Having reached this stage, the person is truly
competent.
I see so many Karate students today who believe that success in
competition is the be all and end all of Karate. To be sure, the sporting
aspect is healthy and enjoyable, but it is not the major part of Karate.
The original idea behind Karate was not to win competitions; not even
to be effective in self defence (though Karate certainly produces this
effectively), but to develop the character and mind of the student.
The true Karateka is unfortunately a rare beast in this day and age. We
have embraced the actions but not the philosophy. John van Weenen is
a true Karateka and consequently, his work is all the more important to
those who are following the "Way". It is not just another manual; it is a
well written, concise insight into Shotokan Karate – a major school of
Japanese Karate.

David Mitchell

Secretary Martial Arts Commission.
Secretary British Karate Federation.
Secretary English Karate Council.
Member of Directing Committee of European Karate Union.
Member of Directing Committee of World Union of Karate
Organisations.

4

KARATE
YESTERDAY AND TODAY

Present day Karate can be traced directly back to the time of Daruma, the Founder of Zen Buddhism. About 1400 years ago, he left Western India on foot for China to give lectures on Buddhism.

His journey of several thousand miles was perilous to say the least, for he had to cross the Himalayas, unbridged rivers, as well as vast stretches of wilderness. He made his journey alone, which gives us a clue to his spiritual as well as physical strength.

In later years, Daruma introduced to his many followers a system of physical movements to improve their strength, following a journey to the Shao-Lin Temple when most of them fell by the way-side from exhaustion.

With this system the Monks of the Shao-Lin Temple came to be known throughout China for their courage and fortitude.

In later times it came to be known as Shorin-Ji Kempo, and this method eventually reached the Ryukyu Islands and developed into Okinawa-Te, the forerunner of present day Karate.

The two Okinawan Masters, Azato and Itosu, were most responsible for teaching and influencing Funakoshi – the father of modern day Karate.

Karate was first introduced to the Japanese public in 1922, when Funakoshi, who was then Professor at the Okinawa Teacher's College, was invited to lecture and demonstrate at an exhibition of Traditional Martial Arts sponsored by the Ministry of Education. His demonstration so impressed the audience that he was flooded with requests to teach in Tokyo.

Instead of returning to Okinawa, Funakoshi taught Karate at various universities, and in 1936 established the Shotokan, a great landmark in the history of Karate in Japan.

In 1955 the Japan Karate Association came into being with Funakoshi as its chief instructor.

Over the years, many of Funakoshi's students have become teachers and masters in their own right, so we see the formation of various styles of Karate, each group basically following Funakoshi's teachings, with its leader developing his own style and technique in accordance with his own "Body System".

Karate has spread to almost every country in the civilised world. It is gaining in popularity everywhere, not only as a Martial Art and Self Defence, but also as a competitive sport.

The latter worries me, for I cannot help feeling that when the J.K.A. arranged and held the first All Japan Karate Championships in 1957, thus putting sport Karate on the map, they had unwittingly grasped the (Shotokan) Tiger by its tail!

5

INTRODUCTION
BASIC TECHNIQUES

The fundamental techniques of Karate are punching, striking, blocking and kicking, and certain considerations need to be observed before they can be performed effectively.

The following factors should be taken into account:

Form – Balance – Centre of Gravity.
Concentration of Power.
Rhythm.
Timing.
Hara – Hips.

Form: Correct form is very important in the execution of Karate techniques as the body must harmonize in order to acquire the stability necessary to sustain the shock of delivering a kick or punch.

Balance: Good balance is essential when performing any Karate technique, especially kicks. At times the body's whole weight must be supported on one leg or transferred quickly from one leg to the other.

Centre of Gravity: Involves Hara, the body's physical and spiritual centre of gravity. Any technique no matter what direction must keep the Hara at a constant level. For example whilst performing Oi Zuki, if at the halfway stage the legs are straightened causing the Hara to rise, and then lowered as the punch is completed, the full power of the technique will not be propelled in a forward direction (towards the opponent).

Concentration of Power: When performing basic techniques the body should remain relaxed and only tensed at the end of the movement when contact is made. This tension is known as "Kime" or focus. Physics dictate that a muscle that is contracted cannot move as quickly as one that is relaxed. Both muscles and tendons should be kept relaxed to allow instant response to changing circumstances. "Kime" is often misunderstood as being "Tensing". "Kime" is relaxing, tensing at the appropriate time and then relaxing.

Rhythm: Is essential in most sports. Think of the poetry of the hurdler or perhaps the butterfly swimmer for example.

In Karate, rhythm is more noticeable in "Kata" and some Karateka have better rhythm than others. Ultimately, a person's "Kinetic" sense is responsible for a Kata being good – or very good.

Rhythm keeps each technique in Kata separate, yet joins them harmoniously together as a whole.

Timing: Good timing is vital and if incorrect, will cause the technique to fail. A punch delivered too soon may be out of range and therefore rendered ineffective, whilst a punch delivered too late may result in no uncertain terms for the executor.

Hara: All body power should emanate from the Hara, the body's natural centre of gravity. If tension is only applied to the muscles of the forearm when punching, the punch will be weak, using only a fraction of the body's capability. Understanding the Hara is the single most important factor in the execution of Karate techniques, for without this knowledge the student will progress up to a point – and no further.
Hips: Coupled with Hara is the Hip movement or "Tanden". When performing basic techniques, the hips should rotate rather than undulate. Of course there are exceptions to this rule as with some kicks but by and large, the mechanics of the hip movement must be appreciated and the laws of action and reaction understood.
The timing of the hips is crucial to the success of the technique.

KATA

Kata is the Japanese word meaning formal exercise and consists of a series of predetermined movements, offensive and defensive, performed consecutively in a set sequence.

The practitioner is fighting four or eight imaginary opponents and to the unenlightened observer, will sometimes resemble a form of shadow boxing.

Until thirty years ago, freestyle contests or engagement matches were unheard of and training consisted mainly of Kata practice. As a result of continually striving to perfect these techniques, Kata, being a contest with oneself, the spirit of Karate-Do prevailed, as it had done for centuries.

About 50 Kata's have come down to us to the present day, these were created by Masters of past generations. The "Type" of movements in the individual Kata gives us a clue to the physical makeup of the Master who created it.

It is probably true to say that Funakoshi did more to systemise the teaching of Kata than any other person.

Kata has many advantages, primarily enabling one to practice alone – anywhere, and without special equipment. As a method of all round exercise, it is almost unbeatable and provides a working knowledge of self defence techniques.

Truly the key to Karate-Do lies within the performance of Kata – and it's there for the taking.

KUMITE

Kumite is the training method where the techniques of defence and attack can be put to practical application. The advantage of training with a partner as opposed to oneself means that, given reasonable control, a student can develop his technique and "Kime" by physically blocking a strong attack.

Kumite training must follow a set pattern, proven over the years. As this book is intended for beginners to 4th Kyu Grade – the following types apply.

Go Hon Kumite – five attack sparring.

Sambon Kumite – three attack sparring.

Kihon Ippon Kumite – basic one attack sparring.

Kaeshi Ippon Kumite – basic one attack (Oi Zuki counter).

Jiyu Ippon Kumite – semi free one attack sparring.

Go Hon Kumite requires the proficiency of formal techniques.

Kihon Ippon Kumite teaches the ability to block and counter strongly – so developing Kime. It also teaches distancing (MAAI). Timing is improved by leaving the block and counter to the last minute.

Jiyu Ippon Kumite is the transitional stage between Kihon Ippon and Jiyu Kumite (free sparring), a complete subject on its own and not covered in this book.

PART 1 KIHON
BASIC TECHNIQUES

The following 84 pages deal exclusively with the more popular basic techniques of Punching, Striking, Blocking and Kicking. All of these techniques can be performed in one or other of the basic Shotokan stances.

As this book is intended for beginners up to 4th Kyu Grade, only the following stances need be mastered, but having said that, students should train hard and endeavour to develop strong stances, as they are mostly the basis for techniques to come.

Zenkutsu Dachi – Front stance.
A strong attacking stance with 70% of the body weight over the front leg.

Kōkutsu Dachi – Back stance.
Used mainly for blocking frontal attacks, having 70% of the body weight over the back leg.

Kiba Dachi – Straddle Leg stance.
Very effective when used in conjunction with side snap or thrust kicks, body weight is evenly spread between both legs.

Fudo Dachi – Rooted stance.
A very strong stance midway between Zenkutsu and Kiba Dachi. The body weight is slightly more forward then back.

Neko Ashi Dachi – Cat stance.
A beautiful stance mainly used in blocking. With 90% of the body weight over the back leg, this stance is ideal for kicking with the front leg.

Left: Shutō Uchi – the moment 10 concrete roof tiles shatter

PUNCHING

Theoretical Considerations for Punching

In basic training, most punches start from the hip but once they have been perfected it may be necessary to punch from any position. Karate punches, in the main, travel in a straight line – the shortest distance between two points – and in an ideal situation, the opposite arm should do the same, in a reverse direction of course. Twisting the wrist on contact aids focus and exhalation. The timing of the beginning of a punch is crucial. If the fist leaves the waist too soon, it will have a pushing effect into its target and be only as strong as the weight or momentum of the person punching allows. Correspondingly, should the punch leave the hip too late, it will never gather momentum in time for it to have any appreciable effect.

Class performing Lunge Punch – during outdoor training session

CHOKU ZUKI
STRAIGHT PUNCH

Choku Zuki is the most basic Karate
punch and is learned in the Hachiji
Dachi stance. The punching hand
begins at the waist in the inverted
position and travels in a straight line to
the target. It stays relaxed, as does the
rest of the body until just
prior to the end of its
travel, when it twists
180° and the whole body
is tensed. The opposite
arm moves in harmony with
the punching arm but of course in the
reverse direction. Contact is made with
Seiken (Fore Fist).

Application

1

2

3

4

15

OI ZUKI
LUNGE PUNCH

Application

Oi Zuki is virtually the same as Choku Zuki but performed whilst stepping forward or back. Starting from the Gedan Barai position bring the rear leg up to the front leg, keeping them both bent at this point, and then carry on forward into the next Zenkutsu Dachi. The arms remain in almost the same position right until the end of the technique and then exchange places, thus utilising fully the snapping action of the arms. At this point the hips should be square on, body tensed and breath exhaled.

2

3

4

GYAKU ZUKI
REVERSE PUNCH

Application

Gyaku Zuki is a technique, usually
performed on the spot, using the
reverse hand to deliver the punch. It is
possibly Karate's strongest punch,
relying very much on applying the
power generated by twisting the hips.
From the Yoi position in Zenkutsu
Dachi with the left hand open, commence
the punch and the withdrawal of the
left arm simultaneously. As in the
photographs opposite it is
important to keep the
hips still in the 45° position as well as
the body (Hanmi) until the second half
of the technique.
As the right hand turns over to punch so
the left inverts and at this point the right
hip is thrust forward to the maximum.
The breath is exhaled and the body
tensed.
The final action of the hands, arms, hips,
body, breathing and tension must
culminate simultaneously.

2

4

MOROTE ZUKI
DOUBLE PUNCH (AUGMENTED)

Application

Morote Zuki begins by having both hands inverted on their respective hips, and in this technique, both arms punch together. Either or both fists make contact – one punching, both punching, or one augmenting the other. During this technique both hips remain fully facing forward and again the body tensed, breath exhaled at the moment of contact.

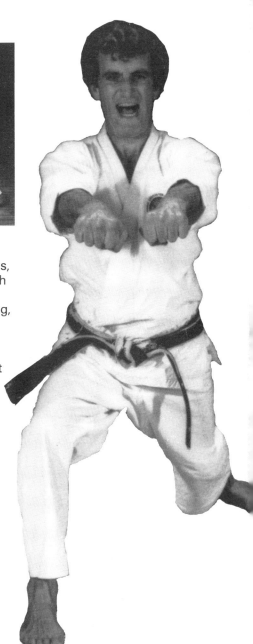

2

4

AGE ZUKI
RISING PUNCH

Application

Age Zuki is a rising punch which makes use of the back of the fist and rises to contact the opponent UNDER the chin It is performed in a similar way to the reverse punch, the main difference being, that the punching arm swings in a wide vertical arc.

As the technique nears its conclusion, the right (reverse) hip is thrust forward the back leg is pushed back and the body tensed whilst exhaling via the mouth.

2

4

23

MAWASHI ZUKI
ROUNDHOUSE PUNCH

Mawashi Zuki may be performed as a
stationary technique (Gyaku) or as a
stepping punch depending on
circumstances.
It follows an outward, circular rising
path culminating in Seiken (Fore Fist)
contacting the temple, at which time
the hips should be rotated accordingly.
The muscles should be tensed and
exhalation takes place via the mouth.

Application

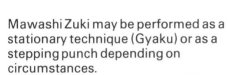

24

2

4

URA ZUKI
CLOSE PUNCH

Ura Zuki is a punch similar to Gyaku Zuki, except the punching arm remains bent on completion and the fist, inverted.
It travels in a straight line and the punch is complete when the punching arm elbow is about six inches from the hip.
Ura Zuki is a lovely "Close In" fighting technique when directed at the Solar Plexus.

Application

26

2

4

TATE ZUKI
VERTICAL PUNCH

Tate Zuki is usually performed as a reverse (Gyaku) technique similar again to Gyaku Zuki. The same straight line is followed but this time, the fist turns only 90° – a quarter turn – and on completion, the punching arm remains slightly bent at the elbow. Exhalation and Kime are the same as preceding techniques.

Application

28

2

4

YAMA ZUKI
U PUNCH

Yama Zuki is a simultaneous multi
level attack. From a left forward stance,
put the right inverted fist by the waist
and bring the left fist over the top of it,
keeping it vertical. From this beginning
position, direct the right fist upward
and forward in a semi-circular fashion
towards the opponent's face.
The right fist finishes with the back of
the fist up, having revolved 180°.
The left fist pushes forward and
inverted, attacks the solar plexus.
Both fists should reach the opponent
together, therefore they should remain
in a vertical line. A slight body
inclination is necessary.

Application

2

4

31

KAGE ZUKI
HOOK PUNCH

Kage Zuki is ideal as a close in fighting body punch but with the fist finishing up in line with your body, it is necessary to step into your opponent to ensure its effectiveness. Used a great deal in Tekki Kata's, this technique is usually performed in Kiba Dachi. Special attention should be given to Kime, especially to the Deltoids and Latissimus Dorsi.

Application

32

2

4

33

STRIKING

Theoretical Considerations for Striking

Striking techniques involve the snapping action of the elbow and rely a great deal on the laws of action and reaction for their power. The force exerted in a striking action is increased by the snapping back effect of the arm, allowing the power of the strike to continue unimpeded to, or through its target. The strike will only be effective if the striking action coincides with the correct application of hips, exhalation and focus. Most strikes serve admirably as blocks too.

Class performing Knife Hand Strike from Heian Yondan, during outdoor training session.

SHUTŌ UCHI
KNIFE HAND STRIKE
(OUTSIDE)

Shutō Uchi (outside) is a semi-circular strike to the neck or temple using the hand edge or "Knife Hand". As illustrated above it can be performed as a reverse technique or as a stepping movement depending on Maai (distancing). In both cases proper use of the hips is essential.

Application

2

4

SHUTŌ UCHI
KNIFE HAND STRIKE (INSIDE)

Shutō Uchi (inside) uses the same part of the hand as the outside technique but commences its movement with the striking hand cupping the opposite ear and the body is practically sideways on at the conclusion of the technique. Contact areas are the neck or temple.

Application

38

2

4

TETTSUI UCHI
BOTTOM FIST STRIKE

Tettsui Uchi can be used to attack most parts of the body. In the case of being grabbed by the wrist, one can use the swinging action of the arm to break the grip and continue over the head, so attacking the opponents skull with Tettsui Uchi.

Application

2

4

41

URAKEN UCHI
BACK FIST STRIKE

Application

Uraken Uchi has basically two forms. The first employs a lateral, semi-circular snapping action focusing the back fist on the opponent's temple. The second involves a semi-circular, overhead strike concentrating the power of the back fist onto the opponent's nose.

The former is a favourite technique for the "Pogo People" for in tournaments, the speed at which it can score can be devastating. A good example of the second occurs in Heian San Dan – or Seienchin.

1

2

3

4

43

HAITO UCHI
RIDGE HAND STRIKE (OUTSIDE)

Haito Uchi or ridge hand strike makes use of the opposite side of the hand to Shutō Uchi. The target area is the temple but make sure the thumb is not protruding out too far otherwise it may get broken. The striking hand swings round the body in a circular motion from a palm up to a palm down position. The beginner should understand straight line techniques before he attempts Haito Uchi, if not, he allows his elbow to go outside the body line when performing basic punches.

Application

44

1

2

3

4

45

HAITO UCHI
RIDGE HAND STRIKE (INSIDE)

Haito Uchi (inside) is often performed from the straddle leg stance, the striking hand moves from palm down to the palm up position and the target area can be the face, temple or neck. On completion of this technique, the body is side on.

Application

46

2

3

4

47

JŌDAN EMPI UCHI
UPPER ELBOW STRIKE

Jōdan Empi Uchi. The effective attacking range is drastically reduced when using elbow attacks as opposed to punches or strikes. Therefore Empi techniques have to be for close encounters. Jōdan Empi Uchi is very similar to Age Uke in many ways – certainly the action and reaction principle is the same. On completion, the elbow should have contacted under the chin and have the back of the fist turned out. Good hip movement is important.

Application

2

3

4

CHŪDAN EMPI UCHI
MIDDLE ELBOW STRIKE

Chūdan Empi Uchi may be performed on the spot as a Gyaku technique or indeed practised as a stepping movement. Either way, the hip movement is of great importance and on completion the attackers index finger knuckle of his striking arm should fit into the small of his chest (touching sternum).

Application

2

4

51

USHIRO CHŪDAN EMPI UCHI
REVERSE MIDDLE ELBOW STRIKE

Application

Ushiro Chūdan Empi Uchi. When attacking in the Gyaku position as in the illustration, the left hip must be back as far as possible so aiding the attacking elbow. The right hand assists for augmenting purposes. It is important to have the left fist facing palm up and the right hip pushed as far forward as possible. The beginner, when practising his first punch, Choku Zuki, inadvertently performs a reverse elbow strike.

2

4

YOKO CHŪDAN EMPI UCHI
SIDE MIDDLE ELBOW STRIKE

Yoko Chūdan Empi Uchi is generally performed in the Kiba Dachi stance and the opponent's sternum makes a fine target for this penetrating technique. On completion, the back of the fist remains up and care should be taken to control very carefully when practising, as sternums have a nasty habit of breaking.

Application

2

4

BLOCKING

Theoretical Considerations for Blocking

Blocking consists of parrying or deflecting blows in such a way as to leave the defender unharmed, and in an advantageous position to counter attack successfully. The attacking limb will have its course altered by the influence of the blocking arm or leg moving in an upwards, downwards or sideways direction.

Advanced training class in progress (Chūdan Uchi Ude Uke)

AGE UKE
UPPER RISING BLOCK

Application

Age Uke is one of the most basic
Shotokan blocks. Points to
remember are these:
The blocking arm should rise
from the waist at an angle of 45°.
The arm and fist turn 180° at the
end of the technique as contact
is made. When pulling the
opposite arm down, make sure
the elbow pulls down in the
direction of the hip. On completion,
the hips and body must be 45° to the
front and the back leg must be
pushed straight on contact.

2

4

SOTO UDE UKE
OUTSIDE FOREARM BLOCK

Application

Soto Ude Uke is perhaps the strongest mid section block of all. On occasions it can be used to block kicks with surprising effectiveness.

The block starts its life at Jōdan level pulled well back past the head. It travels from that position, in a semi circle to a spot roughly in front of the chest and on completion, the wrist turns 180° just prior to Kime. Both body and hips turn 45° into Hanmi.

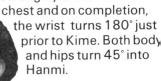

1

2

3

4

61

UCHI UDE UKE
INSIDE FOREARM BLOCK

Application

Uchi Ude Uke is a lot easier to perform than Soto Ude Uke as far as beginners are concerned. The blocking arm starts from above the opposite hip – back of the fist up – and swings in an arc across the body. It finishes its journey in line with the side of the body, the elbow being bent at a 90° angle and the top of the fist in line with the shoulder. The body and hips twist to the 45° position as the block is completed.

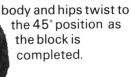

2

4

63

MOROTE UKE
AUGMENTED FOREARM BLOCK

Application

Morote Uke is an inside forward block augmented and strengthened by having the opposite arm to assist it. Indeed, the augmenting arm is quite interesting in so far as it hangs loosely by the side of the body, almost being left behind, then finally accelerates to catch the blocking arm up.
In touching the blocking arm just inside the elbow it strengthens the block quite considerably for it brings into play the muscles on that side of the body and promotes increased harmony.

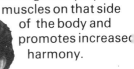

64

2

3

4

SHUTO UKE
KNIFE HAND BLOCK

Application

Shutō Uke – This technique is more difficult than most, therefore it often gets neglected by beginner and high grade alike. Points to remember are: Keep the blocking arm at a 45° angle, otherwise, one may miss the punch completely. The opposite hand should strike the solar plexus as it pulls back. This will assist in Kime. Keep the body and hips at 45° and try not to let the back knee turn in.

2

4

TATE SHUTŌ
VERTICAL KNIFE HAND BLOCK

Application

Tate Shutō is a block utilising the knife hand edge. One needs to be a little more confident when using this technique as opposed to the more conventional blocks. However, once the student has become reasonably accurate, this block will begin to appear more. It can be used to attack inside or outside an opponent's arm and prepares the way for a rapid counter punch.

2

4

JŪJI UKE
X BLOCK (JŌDAN)

Jūji Uke is a very strong double handed blocking technique that can be performed Jōdan or Gedan.
In this, the Jōdan version, the hands rise from the hips at 45° and lock together, crossed above the head. The technique, illustrated here, is called Haishu Jūji Uke, for the back of the hands make contact with the attacker's arm. If performed from a left forward stance, it is important to have the right hip forward as the block concludes.

Application

70

2

4

JŪJI UKE
X BLOCK (GEDAN)

Jūji Uke (Gedan) is a double block used in conjunction with the hips, to stop a front kick and simultaneously attack the shin bone. It really consists of two techniques – Gedan Barai and Tate Zuki. To ensure success, this block needs to be executed quickly, stopping the kicking leg in its tracks and preventing it from gaining speed and momentum.

Application

2

4

73

GEDAN BARAI
DOWNWARD BLOCK

Application

Gedan Barai – The most basic of blocks is probably used and practised more than any other technique. Usually performed in Zenkutsu Dachi, it makes maximum use of the arms, legs, body and hips. Most lessons involve many Gedan Barai's – it's the first technique from the very first Kata and it's still there in the most advanced one. Yes – the left Gedan Barai is most people's strongest block – what about the right one?

2

3

4

KAKIWAKE UKE
WEDGE BLOCK

Application

Kakiwake Uke, the last of our basic blocks is a wedge block, which, after training, is a very effective defence against being grabbed by the coat lapels. Its effective execution depends mainly on being able to contract the Hara and the muscles at the side of the body.

On completion, it leaves the attacker's body wide open and his position is extremely vulnerable, having both hands and arms outside yours.

1

2

3

4

KICKING

Theoretical Considerations for Kicking

Kicking uses the whole of one's body to the maximum and the hips especially play a major role in executing the various techniques. Basically, there are three types of kicks: Snap kicks, thrust kicks and striking kicks. In this book, we have tried to show a representative example from each group but have covered only the basic kicks needed by the beginner.

Snap kicks depend for their success on snapping the leg straight from the knee and then back again as quickly as possible. Once raised, the knee is used as a fulcrum for a semi-circular movement. Thrust kicks rely on raising the knee first and then thrusting the leg straight using the force of the hip for additional power.

Striking kicks may be used for blocking or attacking and their main virtue is flexibility. Balance is a key factor in kicking and keeping the sole of the supporting foot firmly on the floor ensures maximum stability.

A good tip is to aim the knee at the target – the foot should automatically follow.

Class performing Mawashi Geri during outdoor training session

MAE GERI
FRONT KICK

Mae Geri, a front kick
performed from Zenkutsu
Dachi is a snapkick acquiring
its power from the snapping
action of the lower leg aided
by the application of the hips.
Basically there are three positions
that constitute this kick. Firstly, the
kicking leg knee is raised in front and
to the centre of the body. Secondly,
the leg is straightened, hips applied,
instep straightened and toes curled
back.
Thirdly, the leg is snapped back
assuming the first position and with
the hips returned to *their* original
position, the back should be straight
and balance maintained.

Application

2

4

YOKO GERI KEAGE
SIDE SNAP KICK

Yoko Geri Keage is another snap kick but this time the kicking leg travels to the side of the body. Usually performed from a Kiba Dachi, the kicking leg knee is first raised to the side, then the leg is straightened and at this point, the hip rises up to augment the snapping action. Finally, the leg is snapped back – hip lowered and the stance resumed. The striking point is the foot edge (Sokuto).

Application

2

4

83

YOKO GERI KEKOMI
SIDE THRUST KICK

Yoko Geri Kekomi utilises the thrusting action of the leg augmented by the hip. It is more of a "Total Commitment" technique and requires good control and balance keeping the recovery factor in mind. As with Keage, the striking point is Sokuto. An important point to bear in mind is the pivoting action on the ball of the supporting foot as the thrusting takes place. Failure to do this could result in a damaged cartilage in the knee of that supporting leg.

Application

2

4

MAWASHI GERI
ROUNDHOUSE KICK

Mawashi Geri is a semi circular snap kick using the ball of the foot (Koshi) as the striking point. From a Zenkutsu Dachi, raise the knee sideways keeping the leg bent and the toes curled up. Then snap the leg forward aiming the foot at the target, at the same time allowing the hips to rotate. Immediately the leg has straightened, snap it back together with the hips to their original position. At all times endeavour to keep the knee higher than the foot.

Application

2

4

USHIRO GERI
REVERSE KICK

Ushiro Geri makes use of the thrusting action of the leg, aided by the hips in a rearward direction. Usually performed as a spinning technique using the heel as a striking point, Ushiro Geri takes the face of the person kicking furthest away from the attacker and encourages him to commit himself to the technique much more. However, this commitment in competitions may result in disqualification through excessive contact. Both hips should be thrust back simultaneously, as in Oi Zuki or Mae Geri.

Application

88

2

4

URA MIKAZUKI GERI
CRESCENT KICK BLOCK

Ura-Mikazuki-Geri may be used as a block or an attack using the sole of the foot as a striking point. Endeavour to keep the knee parallel to the floor when performing this circular movement.

Application

2

4

MIKAZUKI GERI
CRESCENT KICK

Mikazuki Geri performed as a block or an attack utilises the ball of the foo (Koshi) and the kick take its name from the crescent like action of th leg whether moving in ar inward or outward direction. The thigh of the kicking leg should remai parallel to the floor if possible.

Application

2

3

4

USHIRO MAWASHI GERI
REVERSE ROUNDHOUSE KICK

Ushiro-Mawashi-Geri.
This is a reverse
roundhouse kick using the
heel as the striking point.
Some styles prefer to
contact with the sole of
the foot. This certainly is
the case in tournaments
for obvious reasons.
Bring the kicking leg up
and round, rotating the
hips and body to enable
the heel to make contact
with the back of the
neck or back area
in the case of
Chūdan.

Application

94

2

3

4

KARATE IS FOR
EVERYONE FOR LIFE!

Young children training in Karate

ENJOYED BY YOUNG
AND OLD ALIKE

Older children training in Karate

PART 2 KATA
FORMAL EXERCISE

Kata have been with us for a long time, probably since the Sixth Century. What is remarkable, is that they have endured to this day. True – the techniques may have changed somewhat over the years due to external pressures and influences from the great masters of the past, but the fact remains, they are practised for the same reasons today as they were them. In a nutshell – "The Perfection of Character".
Kata offers so much – to so many by way of physical and mental training.
All the Katas in this book have at least one thing in common – they all begin with defensive movements – to show humility, on the practitioner's part. Their influence overall through physical exercise and breath control directly affect longevity of life. This is borne out by the advanced age to which many masters live.
By continually striving to improve and perfect the techniques in Kata, a person's attitude, mind and character are indirectly improved. Another point often overlooked by many Karateka and one, more profound by far than any other, is this – "a student training in a Dojo, no matter what country, in 1983 could be training in the same techniques as his predecessor was 1,000 years before him. In these days of change and modernisation, how nice it is to be involved in an art *that has truly stood "The Test of Time".*

The following ten elements of Kata as taught by Kanazawa Sensei, must be well practised and understood in order to obtain maximum benefit:

- **Yoi No Kisin** – the spirit of getting ready. The concentration of will and mind against the opponent as a preliminary to the movements of the Kata.
- **Inyo** – the active and passive. Always keeping in mind both attack and defence.
- **Chikara No Kyojaku** – the manner of using strength. The degree of power used for each movement and position in Kata.
- **Waza No Kankyu** – the speed of movement. The speed used for each movement and position in Kata.
- **Tai No Shinshuku** – the degree of expansion or contraction. The degree of expansion or contraction of the body in each movement and position in Kata.
- **Kokyu** – breathing. Breath control related to the posture and movement in Kata.
- **Tyakugan** – the aiming points. In Kata you must keep the purpose of the movement in mind.
- **Kiai** – shouting. Shouting at set points in Kata to demonstrate the martial spirit.
- **Keitai No Hoji** – correct positioning. Correct positioning in movement and stance.
- **Zanshin** – remaining on guard. Remaining on guard at the completion of the Kata (i.e. back to "Yoi") until told to relax "Enoy".

TAIKYOKU SHODAN

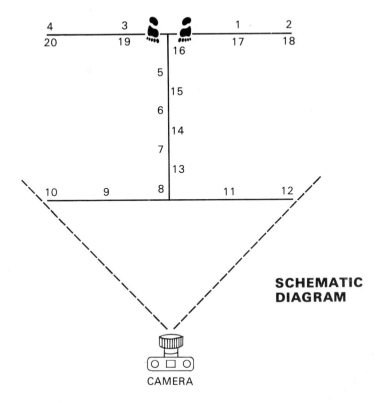

SCHEMATIC DIAGRAM

CAMERA

Of the three Taikyoku forms, Shōdan is the most elementary and consists of one block, one attack and one stance.

Once someone is able to perform the Taikyoku forms with proficiency, he can understand the other Kata with relative ease.

To quote Funakoshi: "Because of its simplicity the Kata is easily learned by beginners, nevertheless, as its name implies*, this form is of the most profound character and one to which, upon mastery of the art of Karate, an expert will return to select it as the ultimate training Kata".

* Taikyoku is a philosophical term denoting the macrocosm before its differentiation into heaven and earth: hence, chaos or the void.

Left: Hidari Gedan Barai

YOI

1

HIDARI GEDAN BARAI

FAST

3

MIGI GEDAN BARAI

FAST

4

HIDARI OI ZUKI

102

2

MIGI OI ZUKI

5

HIDARI GEDAN BARAI

6
MIGI OI ZUKI

7
HIDARI OI ZUKI

9
HIDARI GEDAN BARAI

10
MIGI OI ZUKI

FAST KIAI

8
MIGI OI ZUKI

FAST

11
MIGI GEDAN BARAI

105

FAST

FAST

12

HIDARI OI ZUKI

13

HIDARI GEDAN BARAI

FAST

FAST ⭐ **KIAI**

15

HIDARI OI ZUKI

16

MIGI OI ZUKI

FAST

14

MIGI OI ZUKI

FAST

17

HIDARI GEDAN BARAI

FAST　　　　　　　　　　　　　　**FAST**

18

MIGI OI ZUKI

19

MIGI GEDAN BARAI

YAME

FAST

20

HIDARI OI ZUKI

13-16 FRONT VIEW

FAST   **FAST**

13

HIDARI GEDAN BARAI

14

MIGI OI ZUKI

FAST **KIAI**

16

MIGI OI ZUKI

FAST

15
HIDARI OI ZUKI

APPLICATIONS

A1

A2

B1

B2

C1

C2

TAIKYOKU SHODAN

TAIKYOKU SHODAN

YOI

1

2

6

7

8 KIAI

12

13

14

18

19

20

114

3

4

5

9

10

11

15

16

KIAI

17

YAME

HEIAN SHODAN

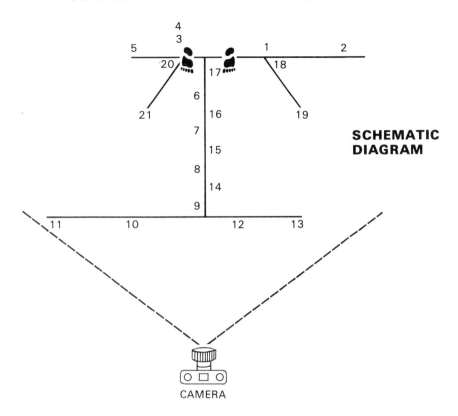

SCHEMATIC DIAGRAM

CAMERA

The word Heian means "Peaceful Mind", Heian Sho Dan being the first of five Heian Katas. It has 21 movements and takes about 40 seconds to perform.

Students should concentrate on perfecting the forward and back stances in this Kata. For the first time, Shutō Uke is introduced together with Age Uke and Tettsui Uchi. Sensei Itosu, the man credited with the compilation of the Heian Katas in the early 1900s set great store in the proficient execution of this Kata.

Left: Migi Jodan Age Uke

117

FAST

YOI

1

HIDARI GEDAN BARAI

FAST

FAST

3

MIGI GEDAN BARAI

4

MIGI TETTSUI UCHI

2
MIGI OI ZUKI

5
HIDARI OI ZUKI

FAST

FAST

6

HIDARI GEDAN BARAI

7

MIGI AGE UKE

FAST **KIAI**

FAST

9

MIGI AGE UKE

10

HIDARI GEDAN BARAI

FAST

8

HIDARI AGE UKE

FAST

11

MIGI OI ZUKI

FAST

FAST

12

MIGI GEDAN BARAI

13

HIDARI OI ZUKI

FAST

FAST

15

MIGI OI ZUKI

16

HIDARI OI ZUKI

FAST

14
HIDARI GEDAN BARAI

FAST **KIAI**

17
MIGI OI ZUKI

123

FAST

18
HIDARI SHUTŌ UKE

FAST

19
MIGI SHUTŌ UKE

FAST

21
HIDARI SHUTŌ UKE

FAST

YAME

20

MIGI SHUTŌ UKE

MOVEMENTS 14·17

FAST

FAST

14
HIDARI GEDAN BARAI

15
MIGI OI ZUKI

FAST

KIAI

17
MIGI OI ZUKI

FAST

16

HIDARI OI ZUKI

APPLICATIONS

HEIAN SHODAN

A3   A4   A5

B2   B3   B4

TAI SABAKI

C4

HEIAN SHODAN

YOI   1   2

6   7   8

12   13   14

18   19   20

KIAI

KIAI

YAME

131

HEIAN NIDAN

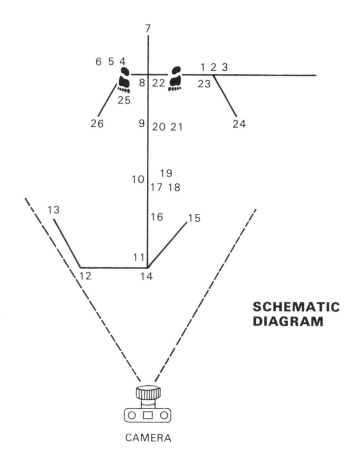

SCHEMATIC DIAGRAM

CAMERA

Heian Nidan carries on where Heian Shodan left off. Having learned the back stance, it is now used to open the Kata and performs in conjunction with Haiwan-Jōdan-Uke. We also see the arrival of techniques like Ura Zuki, Uraken Uchi, Shihon Nukite, and kicking techniques begin to appear in the form of Mae Geri and Yoko Geri. An interesting point concerns the change of direction when executing Yoko Geri Keage.

This Kata requires about 40 seconds to complete the 26 movements.

Left: Migi Chūdan Shihon Nukite

133

YOI

FAST

1
**HIDARI JŌDAN
HAIWAN UKE**

FAST

3
HIDARI CHŪDAN ZUKI

134

FAST

4
**MIGI JŌDAN
HAIWAN UKE**

2

MIGI URA ZUKI

5

HIDARI URA ZUKI

FAST

FAST

6

MIGI CHŪDAN ZUKI

7

YOKO KEAGE-URAKEN

FAST

FAST

9

MIGI SHUTŌ UKE

10

HIDARI SHUTŌ UKE

FAST

8

HIDARI SHUTŌ UKE

FAST  KIAI

11

MIGI CHUDAN SHIHON NUKITE – KIAI

137

FAST

12
HIDARI SHUTŌ UKE

FAST

FAST

13
MIGI SHUTŌ UKE

FAST

15
HIDARI SHUTŌ UKE

FAST

16
| MIGI | GYAKU |
| UCHI UKE | HANM |

138

14

MIGI SHUTŌ UKE

17

**MIGI
MAE GERI**

18

**HIDARI CHŪDAN
GYAKU ZUKI**

19

**HIDARI CHŪDAN
UCHI UKE
GYAKU HANMI**

21

**MIGI CHŪDAN
GYAKU ZUKI**

22

**MIGI CHŪDAN
MOROTE UKE**

140

20

HIDARI MAE GERI

FAST

23

**HIDARI
GEDAN BARAI**

141

FAST

FAST

24

MIGI AGE UKE

25

MIGI GEDAN BARAI

YAME

FAST

26

HIDARI AGE UKE KIAI

15-16 FRONT VIEW

A   B   C   D

17-22 FRONT VIEW

FAST

FAST

17

MIGI MAE GERI

18

HIDARI GYAKU ZUKI

FAST

FAST

20

HIDARI MAE GERI

21

MIGI GYAKU ZUKI

FAST

19

HIDARI UCHI UKE

FAST

22

MIGI MOROTE UKE

145

APPLICATIONS

A1 A2 A3

C1 C2

D1 D2 D3

E4 E5 E6

HEIAN NIDAN

B1 B2 B3

C3 C4

E1 E2 E3

E7 E8 E9

147

HEIAN NIDAN

YOI

1

2

6

7

8

12

13

14

18

19

20

24

25

KIAI

26

3

4

5

9

KIAI

11

15

16

17

21

22

23

YAME

149

HEIAN SANDAN

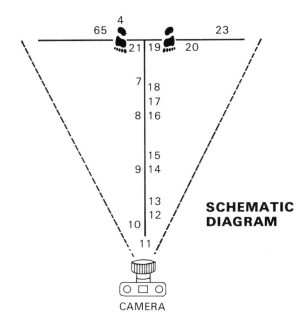

SCHEMATIC DIAGRAM

CAMERA

Heian Sandan begins with Chudan Uchi Uke again performed in Kokutsu Dachi and is followed by Kosa Uke, which in my opinion has been introduced perhaps a little prematurely. Using Kōsa Uke to Block either a Mae Geri or an Oi Zuki is fair enough, despite the degree of difficulty in synchronisation and harmony, however, blocking Yama Zuki is a different kettle of fish and requires much practise together with an ability to "Kime" and relax speedily, ready for the next attack and corresponding Kōsa Uke.

For the first time in Kata, we see the appearance of Fumikomi and Empi Uke and the simultaneous attack of Ushiro Empi and Tate Zuki.

The 21 movements should take 40 seconds to complete.

Left: Hidari Tate Zuki – Migi Empi

YOI

1

**HIDARI CHŪDAN
UCHI UKE**

3

KŌSA UKE

4

MIGI CHŪDAN UCHI UK

152

FAST

2

KŌSA UKE

FAST

5

KŌSA UKE

FAST

6

KŌSA UKE

FAST

7

HIDARI MOROTE UKE

FAST

9

HIDARI TETTSUI UCHI

FAST **KIAI**

10

MIGI CHŪDAN OI ZUKI

8

MIGI SHIHON NUKITE

11

**RYOKEN
KOSHI GAMAE**

FAST

FAST

12
MIGI EMPI UKE

13
JŌDAN URAKEN UCHI

FAST

FAST

15
HIDARI URAKEN UCHI

16
MIGI EMPI UKE

FAST

14

HIDARI EMPI UKE

FAST

17

MIGI URAKEN UCHI

157

SLOW   **FAST**

18

**MIGI CHŪDAN TATE
SHUTO UKE**

19

**HIDARI CHŪDAN
OI ZUKI**

FAST ☆**KIAI**☆

21

**HIDARI TATE ZUKI
MIGI EMPI**

YAME

FAST

20

MIGI TATE ZUKI
HIDARI EMPI

19·20 FRONT VIEW

19

HIDARI CHŪDAN
OI ZUKI

20

MIGI TATE ZUKI
HIDARI EMPI

159

11-19 FRONT VIEW

SLOW

11

RYOKEN KOSHI
GAMAE

FAST

12

MIGI EMPI UKE

FAST

14

HIDARI EMPI UKE

FAST

FAST

15

HIDARI URAKEN UCHI

FAST

17

MIGI URAKEN UCHI

SLOW

18

MIGI CHŪDAN TATE
SHUTO UKE

FAST

13

JŌDAN URAKEN UCHI

FAST

16

MIGI EMPI UCHI

FAST

19

HIDARI CHŪDAN
OI ZUKI

APPLICATIONS

A1 **A2** **A3**

B1 **B2** **B3**

B7 **D1**

C1 **C2** **C3**

HEIAN SANDAN

A4

A5

A6

B4

B5

B6

D2

D3

C4

163

HEIAN SANDAN

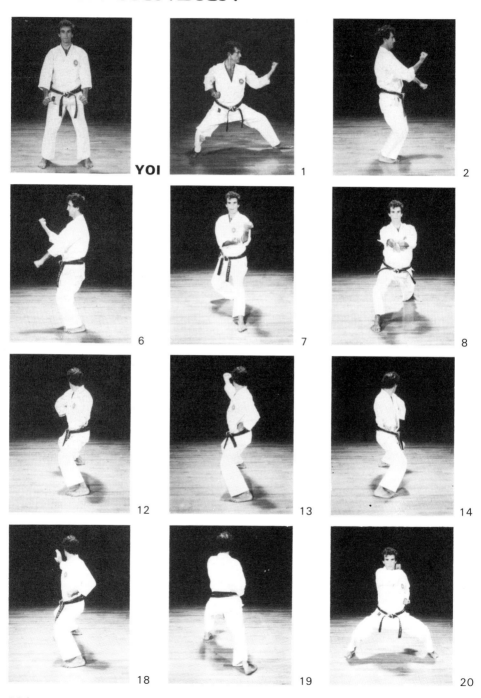

YOI   1   2

6   7   8

12   13   14

18   19   20

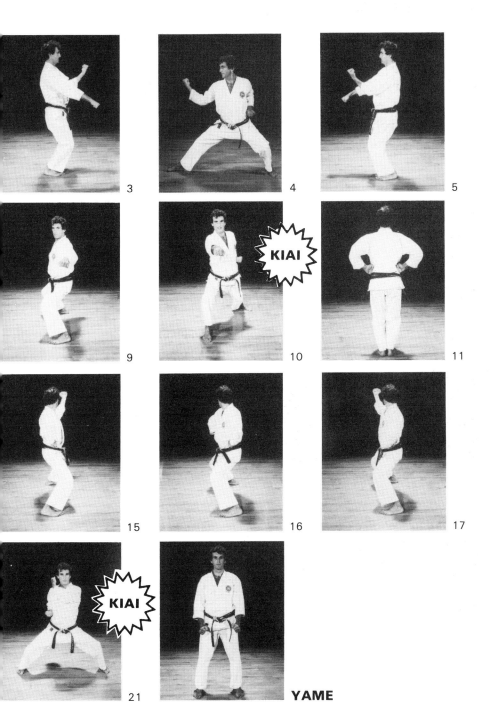

3
4
5
9
10   KIAI
11
15
16
17
21   KIAI
YAME

165

HEIAN YONDAN

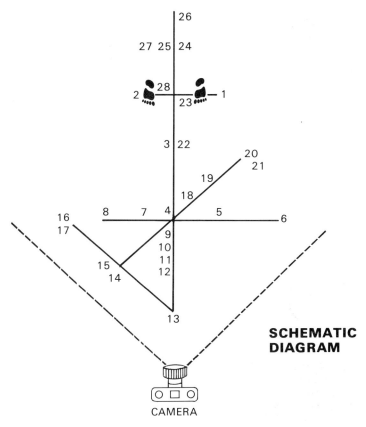

SCHEMATIC
DIAGRAM

CAMERA

Heian Yondan provides the most variation of any Heian Kata and with it, the awareness of the vast number of techniques to be mastered in the future.

Beginning with Haishu Haiwan Uke one learns to harmonise the arms together, develop the power in the block by augmenting one arm with the other, giving the student the opportunity to develop "kime" " through dynamic tension. Appearing for the first time are Juji Uke, Gedan Shutō, Shutō Uchi, Kakiwake Uke and Hiza Geri.

When performing Hiza Geri, equal concentration and power distribution must take place when attacking with the right knee and pulling the head down onto it with both hands. It is important to contract the Hara and use to the optimum the muscles at the side of the body. (Latissimus Dorsi).

Left: Migi Jodan Mae Geri

**SLOW 4–5 SECONDS
LONG INHALATION**

YOI

1

HAISHU HAIWAN UKE

FAST

FAST

3

GEDAN JUJI UKE

4

**MIGI CHŪDAN
MOROTE UKE**

168

SLOW 4–5 SECONDS
LONG INHALATION

2

HAISHU HAIWAN UKE

FAST

5

YOKO KEAGE
URAKEN
UCHI

FAST

FAST

6

MIGI MAE EMPI

FAST

7

**YOKO KEAGE
URAKEN UCHI**

FAST

FAST

9

**HIDARI GEDAN
SHUTŌ BARAI**

FAST

10

**MIGI JŌDAN
SHUTŌ UCHI**

FAST

8

HIDARI MAE EMPI

FAST

11

**MIGI JŌDAN
MAE GERI**

11–12–13 ARE ALL ONE MOVEMENT BUT SHOWN HERE SEPARATELY TO AVOID CONFUSION

FAST

FAST KIAI

12

HIDARI TEISHO UKE

13

MIGI CHŪDAN URAKEN UCHI

FAST

FAST

16

MIGI JŌDAN MAE GERI

MIGI CHŪDAN OI ZUKI

SLOW 4–5 SECONDS
LONG EXHALATION

14

CHŪDAN KAKIWAKE UKE

FAST

17

HIDARI CHŪDAN
GYAKU ZUKI

173

FAST

18

**CHŪDAN KAKIWAKE
UKE**

19

**HIDARI JŌDAN MAE
GERI**

FAST

FAST

21

**MIGI CHŪDAN
GYAKU ZUKI**

22

**HIDARI CHUDAN
MOROTE UKE**

FAST

20

**HIDARI CHŪDAN
OI ZUKI**

FAST

23

**MIGI CHŪDAN
MOROTE UKE**

175

24

**HIDARI CHŪDAN
MOROTE UKE**

25

MOROTE KUBI OSAE

27

**HIDARI CHŪDAN
SHUTŌ UKE**

28

**MIGI CHŪDAN
SHUTŌ UKE**

FAST

KIAI

26

MIGI HIZA GERI UCHI

YAME

21-26 FRONT VIEW

21

**MIGI CHŪDAN
GYAKU ZUKI**

22

**HIDARI CHŪDAN
MOROTE UKE**

FAST

FAST

24

**HIDARI CHŪDAN
MOROTE UKE**

25

MOROTE KUBI OSAE

178

FAST

23

**MIGI CHŪDAN
MOROTE UKE**

FAST **KIAI**

26

**MIGI HIZA
GERI UCHI**

179

APPLICATIONS

BLOCKING   **GRABBING**   **STRIKING**

A1   **A2**   **A3**

BLOCKING   **STRIKING**

B4   **B5**

KICKING

C1

PUNCHING   **PUNCHING**

D3   **D4**

BLOCKING

E1

HEIAN YONDAN

BLOCKING	BLOCKING & STRIKING	KICKING

B1	B2	B3

STRIKING	GRABBING	KICKING

C2	D1	D2

GRABBING	KICKING

E2	E3

HEIAN YONDAN

YOI 1 2

6 7 8

KIAI

12 13 14

18 19 20

24 25 KIAI 26

3

4

5

9

10

11

15

16

17

21

22

23

27

28

YAME

183

HEIAN GŌDAN

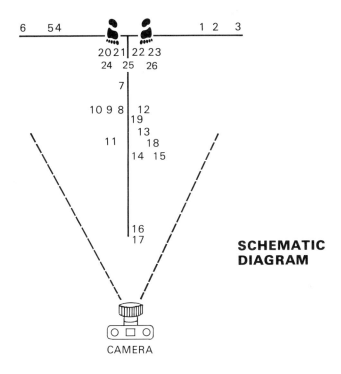

```
6    5 4          2 0 2 1 | 2 2 2 3        1  2   3
                  24  25    26
                       7
                 10 9 8 | 12
                        19
                        13
                 11       18
                 14  15

                        16
                        17
```

SCHEMATIC DIAGRAM

CAMERA

Heian Go Dan introduces the student to many new techniques, none more important than Mizuno-Nagare-No-Kamae – The Flowing Water Technique. This technique is of course for punching but has spiritual connotations. The Forearm, although parallel to the chest, should be inclined slightly downwards with the feeling of water flowing down the arm from the shoulder.

For the first time we see Jōdan Haishu Juji Uke, Morote Tsuki Age and Gedan Nukite.

Jumping over a "Bo" attack to avoid having the legs broken provides an adequate and new experience in Karate movements.

There are 26 movements and they should occupy about 50 seconds.

Left: Migi Mikazuki Geri

YOI

1

HIDARI CHŪDAN UCHI UKE

**LONG INHALATION
SLOW**

3

HIDARI KAGI GAMAE

FAST

4

MIGI CHŪDAN UCHI UKI

186

FAST

2

**MIGI CHŪDAN
GYAKU ZUKI**

FAST

5

**HIDARI CHŪDAN
GYAKU ZUKI**

LONG INHALATION
SLOW

6

MIGI KAGI GAMAE

FAST

7

**MIGI CHŪDAN
MOROTE UKE**

FAST

9

**JODAN HAISHU
JUJI UKE**

FAST

10

CHŪDAN OSAE UKE

FAST

8

GEDAN JUJI UKE

FAST **KIAI**

11

CHŪDAN MIGI OI ZUKI

12

MIGI GEDAN BARAI

13

CHŪDAN HAISHU UKE

FAST

FAST

15

MIGI MAE EMPI

16

**MIGI CHŪDAN
MOROTE UKE**

190

FAST

14

MIGI MIKAZUKI GERI

FAST

17

**KŌHŌ TSUKI
AGE**

18

JUMPING OVER BO

19

GEDAN JŪJI UKE

21

**MIGI GEDAN
SHUTŌ UCHI**

22

**MANJI GAMAE
IN KŌKUTSU DACHI**

20

**MIGI CHŪDAN
MOROTE UKE**

**LONG INHALATION
SLOW**

23

**MANJI GAMAE
IN HEISOKU DACHI**

FAST

FAST

24

**MANJI GAMAE
IN HEISOKU DACHI**

25

**HIDARI GEDAN
SHUTŌ UCHI**

27

YAME

194

FAST

26

**MANJI GAMAE
IN KŌKUTSU DACHI**

19-20 FRONT VIEW

FAST   **FAST**

GEDAN JUJI UKE

**MIGI CHŪDAN
MOROTE UKE**

11-12 SIDE VIEW

FAST   **FAST**

KIAI

CHŪDAN MIGI OI ZUKI

MIGI GEDAN BARAI

196

APPLICATIONS

YOI	BLOCKING	PUNCHING
A1	A2	A3

BLOCKING A KICK	BLOCKING A PUNCH	BLOCKING A PUNCH
B1	B2	B3

PUSHING BACK	PUNCHING
B4	B5

APPLICATIONS

READY TO ATTACK
BLOCKING
BLOCKING

C1

C2

C3

BLOCKING
PUNCHING

E1

E2

E3

BLOCKING
BLOCKING & STRIKING
GRABBING

G1

G2

G3

HEIAN GODAN

BLOCKING

KICKING

STRIKING

D1

D2

D3

JUMPING OVER BO

F1

F2

F3

BLOCKING

F4

BREAKING GRIP

G4

HEIAN GODAN

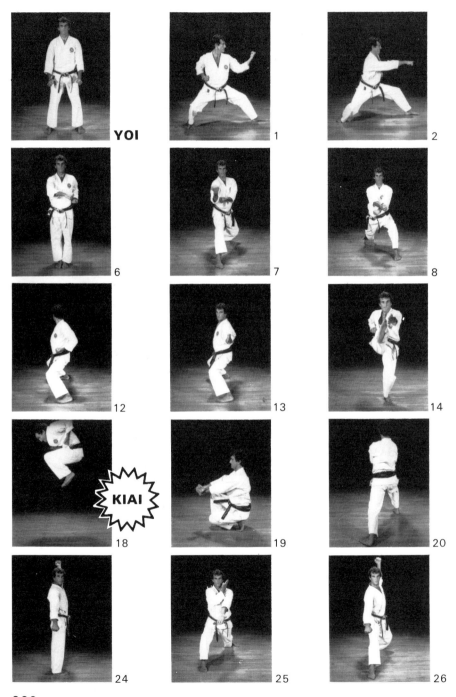

YOI

1

2

6

7

8

12

13

14

KIAI

18

19

20

24

25

26

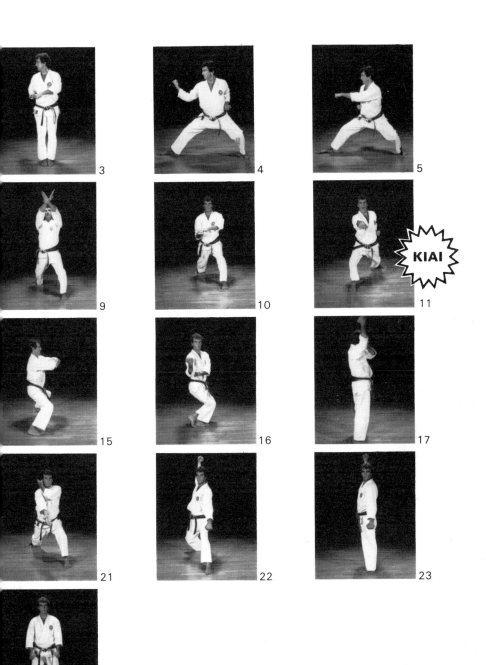

YAME

PART 3 KUMITE
SPARRING

The following pages show the step-by-step method of learning the various types of Kumite that eventually lead up to Jiyu Kumite (Free Style Sparring).

Each of the three, Go Hon Kumite, Sambon Kumite and Kihon Ippon Kumite are of great importance if the Karateka wishes to become proficient in Jiyu Kumite.

Today, more and more people are being attracted to Karate for what I consider the wrong reasons. Let me put it another way – people are being attracted to the Sport not the Art.

A contest should be about neither winning nor losing but participation. Many people enter competitions today for the wrong reasons.

Tournaments bring out a person's ego quite often and that person loves to hear the roar of the crowd, wants to receive a big cash prize or silver trophy, and on occasions like this – it's hard to spot humility, or the many other attributes the Martial Art inspires.

Karate is a fighting art and Kumite is an intrinsic part of it. Jiyu Kumite is a part of overall Karate training, but let's keep things in perspective – it's just a part – and no more.

The moment a Gyaku Zuki scores

GO HON KUMITE
5 ATTACK SPARRING

Go Hon Kumite is the first Kumite practise in Shotokan. It consists of
five attacks (stepping), five defences and a counter attack.
Go Hon Kumite is designed to develop strong attacks and strong blocks
and teach control on the counter attack.
It also helps the beginner begin to appreciate such factors as timing,
distancing and breathing.
Up until this time in basic training, the student has only performed his
techniques in mid air, now he has a face or stomach to aim at, and this
helps from the point of view of accuracy.
Finally, all the techniques are pre-arranged and there is one Kiai on the
counter attack.

Left: Hidari Jōdan Age Uke

No. 1 JŌDAN

TRAINING METHOD FOR GO HON KUMITE (WITHOUT PARTNER)

STEPPING →

START

| YOI | GEDAN BARAI | OI ZUKI | OI ZUKI |

**FROM YOI STEP BACK
INTO GEDAN BARAI**

← STEPPING BACK

FINISH

| YOI | RIGHT GYAKU ZUKI | AGE UKE | AGE UKE |

**AFTER GYAKU ZUKI
STEP BACK INTO
YOI POSITION**

FORWARD

| OI ZUKI | OI ZUKI | OI ZUKI | YOI |

**AFTER 5TH OI ZUKI
STEP FORWARD INTO
YOI POSITION**

STEPPING BACK

| AGE UKE | AGE UKE | AGE UKE | YOI |

No. 2 CHŪDAN

TRAINING METHOD FOR GO HON KUMITE (WITHOUT PARTNER)

STEPPING

START

YOI	GEDAN BARAI	OI ZUKI	OI ZUKI

FROM YOI STEP BACK INTO GEDAN BARAI

STEPPING

FINISH

YOI	GYAKU ZUKI	SOTO UKE	SOTO UKE

AFTER GYAKU ZUKI STEP BACK INTO YOI POSITION

FORWARD →

FINISH

| OI ZUKI | OI ZUKI | OI ZUKI | YOI |

AFTER 5TH ZUKI
STEP FORWARD INTO
YOI POSITION

BACK ←

START

| SOTO UKE | SOTO UKE | SOTO UKE | YOI |

No. 3 MAE GERI
TRAINING METHOD FOR GO HON KUMITE (WITHOUT PARTNER)

STEPPING →

START

YOI

FROM YOI STEP
BACK INTO
ZENKUTSU DACHI

FORWARD STANCE

MAE GERI

MAE GERI

← STEPPING

FINISH

YOI

GYAKU ZUKI

AFTER GYAKU ZUKI
STEP BACK INTO
YOI POSITION

GEDAN BARAI

GEDAN BARAI

210

FORWARD

FINISH

| MAE GERI | MAE GERI | MAE GERI | YOI |

**STEP FORWARD
INTO YOI POSITION**

BACK

START

| GEDAN BARAI | GEDAN BARAI | GEDAN BARAI | YOI |

**FROM YOI POSITION
STEP BACK**

GO HON KUMITE

YOI

ATTACKER STEPS BACK
GEDAN BARAI

MIGI   3   HIDARI
OI ZUKI   AGE UKE

HIDARI   4   MIGI
OI ZUKI   AGE UKE

212

JŌDAN ATTACK

MIGI	1	HIDARI	HIDARI	2	MIGI
OI ZUKI		AGE UKE	OI ZUKI		AGE UKE

MIGI	5	HIDARI	COUNTER ATTACK RIGHT
OI ZUKI		AGE UKE	GYAKU ZUKI (KIAI)

**AFTER, BOTH MOVE IN THIS
DIRECTION** ──────▶

213

GO HON KUMITE

YOI

ATTACKER STEPS BACK
GEDAN BARAI

MIGI 3 HIDARI
OI ZUKI SOTO UDE UKE

HIDARI 4 MIGI SOTO
OI ZUKI UDE UKE

CHŪDAN ATTACK

| MIGI | 1 | HIDARI |
| OI ZUKI | | SOTO UDE UKE |

| MIGI | 2 | MIGI SOTO |
| OI ZUKI | | UDE UKE |

| MIGI | 5 | HIDARI |
| OI ZUKI | | SOTO UDE UKE |

COUNTER ATTACK
CHUDAN GYAKU ZUKI (KIAI)

AFTER, BOTH MOVE IN THIS DIRECTION ⟶

GO HON KUMITE

YOI

ATTACKER STEPS BACK
IN ZENKUTSU DACHI

MIGI   3   HIDARI
MAE GERI   GEDAN BARAI

HIDARI   4   MIGI
MAE GERI   GEDAN BARA

MAE GERI ATTACK

MIGI	1	HIDARI	HIDARI	2	MIGI
MAE GERI		GEDAN BARAI	MAE GERI		GEDAN BARAI

MIGI   5   **HIDARI**
MAE GERI   **GEDAN BARAI**

COUNTER ATTACK WITH
RIGHT GYAKU ZUKI

AFTER, BOTH MOVE IN THIS
DIRECTION ——————→

SAMBON KUMITE
3 LEVEL ATTACK SPARRING

Sambon Kumite or three-attack sparring can be performed in the same way as Go Hon Kumite, with the resulting benefits of developing strong blocks and attacks, together with improvement in "Kime".

On the other hand, Sambon Kumite may take the form of a multi-level sequence so providing pre arranged variation in attack and defence.

On the following pages, the reader will see this form demonstrated in the simple form of Jōdan Oi Zuki, Chūdan Oi Zuki and Chūdan Mae Geri attacks being countered with Age Uke, Soto Ude Uke, Mae Geri and Gyaku Zuki.

Once this simple routine has been perfected, there are no end to the number of hand and foot combinations that can be utilised.

As no attack and defence is usually repeated twice, Sambon Kumite prepares the students' mind for change and encourages him to think quickly.

Shortly he will advance to Kihon Ippon Kumite and its multitude of contrasting techniques, however – firstly he *must* master Sambon Kumite.

Left: Hidari Chūdan Soto Ude Uke

219

TRAINING METHOD FOR SAMBON KUMITE (WITHOUT PARTNER)

START

**FROM YOI ATTACKER STEPS
BACK INTO GEDAN BARAI**

FINISH

**STEP BACK INTO
YAME POSITION**

2 **STEP FORWARD** 3
INTO YAME POSITION

**FROM YOI POSITION
STEP BACK**

SAMBON KUMITE

YOI

ATTACKER STEPS BACK
GEDAN BARAI

MAE GERI   3   HIDARI
CHŪDAN   GEDAN BARAI

COUNTER ATTACK
GYAKU ZUKI CHŪDAN

AFTER, BOTH MOVE IN THIS
DIRECTION ⟶

3 LEVEL ATTACK SPARRING

OI ZUKI 1 **HIDARI**
JŌDAN **AGE UKE**

OI ZUKI 2 **MIGI SOTO**
CHŪDAN **UDE UKE**

YAME

KIHON IPPON KUMITE
BASIC ONE ATTACK SPARRING

Sometimes called the Basic Kata of Sparring, Kihon Ippon Kumite, or basic 1-attack sparring, allows both persons to take it in turn attacking with pre-arranged techniques and defending and counter attacking.

One learns about "Maai" (Distancing) very early on and the fact that it is not necessary always to defend in straight lines. It is possible to move in other directions and parry the attacker rather than use brute force. Consequently, side stepping and moving at 45° lend themselves admirably for this purpose.

Kihon Ippon Kumite begins with the attacker in Gedan Barai and the defender in the Yoi position. The person defending having completed his counter attack with Kiai, then returns to the Yoi position. He does not pull into the free style "Kamae" pose in any circumstances.

Kihon Ippon Kumite is the formal exercise of sparring and should not be confused with Jiyu Ippon Kumite (semi free 1 attack sparring).

The attacker should attack strongly at all times, exercising control to the face but making some contact if possible when attacking to the mid section.

The defender, after blocking, should focus his counter attack just short of the target and on no account follow through and make contact.

When training in basics in a class situation we always step FORWARD into Gedan Barai. This is to show martial spirit. However, when training with a partner, as in Kihon Ippon Kumite, we always step BACK into Gedan Barai, thus showing humility and gratitude for having someone to train with.

Bowing ("Rei") before training together and after, signifies mutual respect.

Left: Jōdan Shuto Uchi

JŌDAN ATTACKS No. 1

SHIZENTAI 1 **HIDARI GEDAN BARAI**

HIDARI JŌDAN AGE UKE 3 **MIGI JŌDAN OI ZUKI**

HIDARI JŌDAN AGE UKE   2   **MIGI JŌDAN OI ZUKI**
(HALFWAY)   **(HALFWAY)**

MIGI CHŪDAN GYAKU ZUKI   4   **MIGI JŌDAN OI ZUKI**

JŌDAN No. 2

SHIZENTAI   1   HIDARI GEDAN BARAI

HIDARI JŌDAN TATE SHUTŌ UKE   3   MIGI JŌDAN OI ZUKI

IIDARI JŌDAN TATE SHUTŌ UKE 2   **MIGI JŌDAN OI ZUKI**
(HALFWAY)   **(HALFWAY)**

MIGI JŌDAN SHUTŌ UCHI   4   **MIGI JŌDAN OI ZUKI**

JŌDAN No. 3

SHIZENTAI 1 **HIDARI GEDAN BARAI**

MIGI YOKO GERI KEAGE 3 **MIGI JŌDAN OI ZUKI**

MIGI JŌDAN AGE UKE   2   **MIGI JŌDAN OI ZUKI**
IN HEISOKU DACHI

MIGI CHŪDAN YOKO EMPI   4   **MIGI JŌDAN OI ZUKI**

JŌDAN No. 4

SHIZENTAI   1   **HIDARI GEDAN BARAI**

MIGI CHŪDAN MAWASHI GERI   3   **MIGI JŌDAN OI ZUKI**

HAISHU JŪJI UKE   2   **MIGI JŌDAN OI ZUKI**

HIDARI USHIRO MAWASHI EMPI 4   **MIGI JŌDAN OI ZUKI**

CHŪDAN ATTACKS No. 1

SHIZENTAI   1   **HIDARI GEDAN BARAI**

HIDARI CHŪDAN SOTO UDE UKE 3   **MIGI CHŪDAN OI ZUKI**

HIDARI CHŪDAN SOTO UDE UKE 2   **MIGI CHŪDAN OI ZUKI**
(HALFWAY)   **(HALFWAY)**

MIGI CHŪDAN GYAKU ZUKI   4   **MIGI CHŪDAN OI ZUKI**

235

CHŪDAN No. 2

SHIZENTAI   1   **HIDARI GEDAN BARAI**

MIGI CHŪDAN SOTO UDE UKE   3   **MIGI CHŪDAN OI ZUKI**

MIGI CHŪDAN SOTO UDE UKE   2   **MIGI CHŪDAN OI ZUKI**
(HALFWAY)   **(HALFWAY)**

MIGI CHŪDAN YOKO EMPI   4   **MIGI CHŪDAN OI ZUKI**

237

CHŪDAN No. 3

SHIZENTAI   1   HIDARI GEDAN BARAI

HIDARI JŌDAN KIZAMI ZUKI   3   MIGI CHŪDAN OI ZUKI

HIDARI CHŪDAN UCHI UDE UKE 2   **MIGI CHŪDAN OI ZUKI**

MIGI CHŪDAN GYAKU ZUKI   4   **MIGI CHŪDAN OI ZUKI**

CHŪDAN No. 4

SHIZENTAI   1   HIDARI GEDAN BARAI

HIDARI CHŪDAN KIZAMI MAE GERI   3   MIGI CHŪDAN OI ZUKI

HIDARI CHŪDAN SHUTO UKE 2 **MIGI CHŪDAN OI ZUKI**

MIGI CHŪDAN NUKITE 4 **MIGI CHŪDAN OI ZUKI**

241

MAE GERI ATTACKS No. 1

SHIZENTAI   1   **HIDARI ZENKUTSU DACHI**

HIDARI GEDAN BARAI   3   **MIGI CHŪDAN MAE GERI**

HIDARI GEDAN BARAI   2   **MIGI CHŪDAN MAE GERI**
(HALFWAY)   **(HALFWAY)**

MIGI CHŪDAN GYAKU ZUKI   4   **MIGI ZENKUTSU DACHI**

MAE GERI No. 2

SHIZENTAI   1   HIDARI ZENKUTSU DACHI

HIDARI JŌDAN KIZAMI ZUKI   3

MIGI GEDAN BARAI   2   **MIGI CHŪDAN MAE GERI**
GYAKU HANMI

MIGI CHŪDAN GYAKU ZUKI   4   **MIGI ZENKUTSU DACHI**

245

MAE GERI No. 3

SHIZENTAI   1   HIDARI ZENKUTSU DACHI

PULLING BACK   3   MIGI ZENKUTSU DACHI
(HALFWAY POINT)

GEDAN JŪJI UKE   2   **MIGI CHŪDAN MAE GERI**

JŌDAN SHUTŌ JUJI UKE   4   **MIGI ZENKUTSU DACHI**
(A BLOCK USED AS AN ATTACK)

MAE GERI No. 4

SHIZENTAI   1   **HIDARI ZENKUTSU DACHI**

HIDARI CHŪDAN TATE SHUTŌ UKE 3   **MIGI CHŪDAN**
MIGI NEKO ASHI DACHI   **MAE GERI SNAPPING BACK**

MIGI GEDAN BARAI   2   **MIGI CHŪDAN MAE GERI**
MIGI NEKO ASHI DACHI

MIGI CHŪDAN MAE EMPI   4

YOKO GERI KEKOMI ATTACKS No.

SHIZENTAI   1   **HIDARI ZENKUTSU DACHI**

HIDARI CHŪDAN SOTO   3   **MIGI CHŪDAN YOKI**
UDE UKE   **GERI KEKOMI**

HIDARI CHŪDAN SOTO   2   **MIGI CHŪDAN YOKO**
UDE UKE (HALFWAY)   **GERI KEKOMI (HALFWAY)**

MIGI CHŪDAN GYAKU ZUKI   4

KEKOMI No. 2

SHIZENTAI 1 **HIDARI ZENKUTSU DACHI**

HIDARI GEDAN KAKE UKE 3 **MIGI CHŪDAN YOKO GERI KEKOMI**

252

HIDARI GEDAN KAKE UKE 2 **MIGI CHŪDAN YOKO**
(HALFWAY) **GERI KEKOMI (HALFWAY)**

MIGI JŌDAN HAITO UCHI 4

253

MAWASHI GERI ATTACKS No. 1

1   **HIDARI ZENKUTSU DACHI**

HIDARI JŌDAN UCHI UDE UKE   3   **MIGI JŌDAN MAWASHI GERI**

254

HIDARI JŌDAN UCHI UDE UKE 2 **MIGI JŌDAN MAWASHI GERI**
(HALFWAY) **(HALFWAY)**

MIGI CHŪDAN GYAKU ZUKI 4

MAWASHI GERI No. 2

1   **HIDARI ZENKUTSU DACHI**

MIGI JŌDAN MAWASHI GERI   3   **JŌDAN SHUTŌ MOROTE UKE**

JŌDAN SHUTŌ MOROTE UKE   2   **MIGI JŌDAN MAWASHI GERI**
(HALFWAY)   **(HALFWAY)**

MIGI CHŪDAN MOROTE YOKO EMPI 4

257

THE DOJO KUN
MORALS OF THE DOJO

The "Dojo Kun" is the Oath of the Karateka. Even today, it is recited at the end of each lesson at the Tokyo Headquarters of the Japan Karate Association, along with other Dojos in the J.K.A. Outside Japan I have not heard it, other than at training sessions of the Traditional Association of Shotokan Karate in Great Britain.

At the end of each lesson, the students and instructors line up to take the formal bow or "Rei", but before this and the usual "Mokuso" period, the whole class will sit in "Seiza" facing a shrine dedicated to Funakoshi Sensei.

The Dojo Captain or Senior Grade at the end of the two lines will shout out the "Dojo Kun", line at a time and immediately, the whole class will repeat each line back.

The Oath should always be chanted with strength, never mumbled in insincerity, for just as Karate movements should become automatic and reflexes conditioned, the simple Truths of the Oath should also penetrate the mind of the participant.

The "Dojo Kun" embodies all we are trying to achieve through the physical efforts of Karate training.

"THE DOJO KUN"

"Dojo Kun"

"Hitotsu! Jinkaku Kansei ni Tsutomuru Koto"
(One! To Strive For The Perfection of Character!)

"Hitotsu! Makoto No Michi O Mamoru Koto!"
(One! To Defend The Paths Of Truth!)

"Hitotsu! Doryoku No Seishin O Yashinau Koto!
(One! To Foster The Spirit Of Effort!)

"Hitotsu! Reigi O Omonzuru Koto!"
(One! To Honour The Principles of Etiquette!)

"Hitotsu! Kekki No Yu O Imashimuru Koto!"
(One! To Guard Against Impetuous Courage!)

There now follows details of the official grading syllabus as laid down
by the Traditional Association of Shotokan Karate. It is offered purely
as a guide to maintaining examination standards.

T.A.S.K.

OFFICIAL GRADING
SYLLABUS

GRADING SYLLABUS
CONTENTS

The Traditional Association of Shotokan Karate is affiliated to the English Karate Federation, the Martial Arts Commission and the World Union of Karate Organisations

T.A.S.K. Chief Instructor and Examiner:
Sensei J. van Weenen 5th Dan

9th KYU – RED BELT

Command

	Kara-tzuki × 10
Both sides	Gyaku-tzuki × 5
	Oi-tzuki × 5
Turn	Age-uke × 5
Turn	Ude-uke × 5
Turn	Uchi-uke × 5
	Mae-geri × 5
Both sides	Keage × 3
Both sides	Kekomi × 3
	Gohon Kumite (Jōdan and Chūdan)
	Taikyo-ku Kata

8th KYU – ORANGE BELT

Command

	Kara-tzuki × 10
Both Sides	Gyaku-tzuki × 5
	Oi-tzuki × 5
Forward + back	Age-uke × 5
Forward + back	Ude-uke × 5
Forward + back	Uchi-uke × 5
Forward + back	Shutō-uke × 5
	Mae-geri × 5
Both sides	Keage × 3
Both sides	Kekomi × 3

Gohon Kumite
Jōdan and Chūdan

Kata
Heian Shodan

262

7th KYU – YELLOW BELT

Command		
	Oi-tzuki × 5	*Lunge Punch*
Forward + back	Age-uke/Gyaku-tzuki × 5	*Rising Block / Reverse Pnd*
Forward + back	Ude-uke/Gyaku-tzuki × 5	*Outside Forearm Block*
Forward + back	Uchi-uke/Gyaku-tzuki × 5	*Inside Forearm Block*
Forward + back	Shutō-uke/Nukite × 5	*Knife Hand Strike / Spear Hand*
	Mae-geri × 5	
Both sides	Keage × 3	*Knee side*
Both sides	Kekomi × 3	*Knee front*

Kihon-Ippon Kumite

Both sides	2 × Jōdan
Both sides	2 × Chūdan

Kata
Heian Nidan

6th KYU – GREEN BELT

Command	
	Sanbon-tzuki × 5
Turn	Sanbon-tzuki × 5
Forward + back	Age-uke/Gyaku-tzuki/Gedan-barai × 5
Forward + back	Ude-uke/Gyaku-tzuki/Gedan-barai × 5
Forward + back	Uchi-uke/Gyaku-tzuki/Gedan-barai × 5
Forward + back	Shut-uke/Mae-geri (front leg)/Nukite × 5
	Mae-geri × 5
Turn	Mae-geri × 5
Both sides	Keage × 3
	Kekomi (In Zen-Kutsu-dachi) × 3
	Ren-geri, Mae-geri Chūdan/Jōdan × 3
Turn	Ren-geri, Mae-geri Chūdan/Jōdan × 3
	Mawashi-geri × 3

Kihon-Ippon Kumite

Both sides	2 × Jōdan
Both sides	2 × Chūdan
Both sides	2 × Mae-geri
Both sides	2 × Kekomi

Kata
Heian Sandan, plus any previous kata

5th KYU – PURPLE BELT

Command

	Sanbon-tzuki × 5
Step back	Sanbon-tzuki × 5
Forward+back	Age-uke/Mae-geri/Gyaku-tzuki × 5
Forward+back	Ude-uke/Empi/Uraken × 5
Forward+back	Uchi-uke/Kizami-tzuki/Gyaku-tzuki × 5
Forward+back	Shutō-uke/Mae-geri (front leg)/Nukite × 5
	Mae-geri/Oi-tzuki × 5
Turn	Mae-geri/Gyaku-tzuki × 5
	Ren-geri, Mae-geri Chūdan/Jōdan × 5
Turn	Ren-geri, Mae-geri Chūdan/Jōdan × 5
	Ren-geri, Mae-geri/Mawashi-geri × 3
Turn	Ren-geri, Mae-geri/Mawashi-geri × 3
	Ren-geri, Mae-geri/Kekomi × 3
Turn	Ren-geri, Mae-geri/Kekomi × 3

*Kihon-Ippon Kumite**

Both sides	2 × Jōdan
Both sides	2 × Chūdan
Both sides	2 × Mae-geri
Both sides	2 × Kekomi

Kata
Heian Yondan, plus any previous kata

* The same defence must not be repeated on the same side

4th KYU – PURPLE + WHITE BELT

Command	
	Sanbon-tzuki × 5
Turn	Sanbon-tzuki/Mae-geri/Sanbon-tzuki × 5
Forward + back	Age-uke/Mai-geri/Gyaku-tzuki/Gedan-barai × 5
Forward + back	Ude-uke/Empi/Uraken/Gyaku-tzuki/ Gedan-barai × 5
Forward + back	Uchi-uke (Ko Kutsu-dachi)/Kizami-tzuki/ Gyaku-tzuki/Gedan-barai × 5 Gedan-barai × 5
Forward + back	Shutō-uke/Mae-geri (front leg)/Nukite × 5 Mae-geri/Mawashi-geri/Uraken/ Gyaku-tzuki/Gedan-barai × 5
Turn	Mae-geri/Mawashi-geri/Uraken/ Gyaku-tzuki/Gedan-barai × 5 Mae-geri–Kekomi/Shuto-uchi/ Gyaku-tzuki/Gedan-barai × 3
Turn	Mae-geri–Kekomi/Shutō-uchi/ Gyaku-tzuki/Gedan-barai × 3
Both sides	Keage (Kiba-dachi)/Gyaku-tzuki (Zen Kutsu-Dachi)/Gedan-barai (Kiba-dachi) × 3 *Kaeshi-Ippon Kumite*

From the Gedan-barai position the first person attacks Jodan Oi-tzuki, the second person defends Age-uke, and counters Chudan Oi-tzuki, the first person defends by stepping back and blocking Ude-uke and countering Gyaku-tzuki. This technique to be performed twice each side by both people.

*Kihon-Ippon Kumite**

Both sides	2 × Jōdan
Both sides	2 × Chūdan
Both sides	2 × Mae-geri
Both sides	2 × Kekomi
Both sides	2 × Mawashi-geri

Kata
Heian Godan, plus any previous kata

* The same defence must not be repeated on the same side

3rd KYU – BROWN BELT

Command

	Sanbon-tzuki × 5
Turn	Sanbon-tzuki/Mae-geri/Sanbon-tzuki × 5
Forward + Back	Age-uke/Mae-geri/Gyaku-tzuki/Gedan-barai × 5
Forward + Back	Ude-uke/Empi/Uraken/Gyaku-tzuki/Gedan-barai × 5
Forward + Back	Uchi-uke (Kokutsu-dachi)/Kizami-tzuki/ Gyaku-tzuki/Gedan-barai × 5
Forward + Back	Shutō-uke/Mae-geri (front leg)/Nukite × 5 Mae-geri/Mawashi-geri/Uraken/ Gyaku-tzuki/Gedan-barai × 5
Turn	Mae-geri/Mawashi-geri/Uraken/ Gyaku-tzuki/Gedan-barai × 5 Mae-geri/Kekomi/Shutō-uchi/Gyaku-tzuki/Gedan-barai × 5
Turn	Mae-geri/Kekomi/Shutō-uchi/Gyaku-tzuki/Gedan-barai × 5
Both sides	Keage (Kiba-dachi)/Gyaku-tzuki (Zenkutsu-dachi)/Gedan-barai (Kiba-dachi) × 3 Ushiro-geri × 3
Both sides	Face the front; Mae-geri/Kekomi, with the same leg

Jiyu-Ippon Kumite

One side only	2 × Jōdan
One side only	2 × Chūdan
One side only	2 × Mae-geri

and Kihon-Ippon Kumite *

Both sides	2 × Jōdan
Both sides	2 × Chūdan
Both sides	2 × Mae-geri

* The same defence must not be repeated on the same side.

Kata
Tekki-Shodan, plus any other previous kata

2nd KYU – BROWN + WHITE BELT

Command	
	Sanbon-tzuki × 5
Turn	Sanbon-tzuki/Mae-geri/Sanbon-tzuki × 5
Forward + Back	Age-uke/Mae-geri/Gyaku-tzuki/Gedan-barai × 5
Forward + Back	Uke-uke/Empi/Uraken/Gyaku-tzuki/ Gedan-barai × 5
Forward + Back	Uchi-uke (Kokutsu-dachi)/Kizami-tzuki/ Gyaku-tzuki/Gedan-barai × 5
Forward + Back	Shutō-uke/Mawashi-geri (Front leg)/Nukite × 5
	Mae-geri/Mawashi-geri/Uraken/ Gyaku-tzuki/Gedan-barai × 5
Turn	Mae-geri/Mawashi-geri/Uraken/ Gyaku-tzuki/Gedan-barai × 5
	Mae-geri/Kekomi/Shutō-uchi/ Gyaku-tzuki/Gedan-barai × 5
Turn	Mae-geri/Kekomi/Shutō-uchi/ Gyaku-tzuki/Gedan-barai × 5
Both sides	Keage (Kiba-dachi)/Gyaku-tzuki (Zenkutsu-dachi/)/Gedan-barai (Kiba-dachi)
	Ushiro-geri/Gyaku-tzuki × 5
Turn	Ushiro-geri/Gyaku-tzuki × 5
Both sides	Face the front; Mae-geri/Kekomi, with the same leg × 5
Both sides	Face the front; Mae-geri/Mawashi-geri, with the same leg × 5

Jiyu-Ippon Kumite	
Both sides	2 × Jōdan
Both sides	2 × Chūdan
Both sides	2 × Mae-geri

and Kihon-Ippon Kumite *	
Both sides	2 × Jōdan
Both sides	2 × Chūdan
Both sides	2 × Mae-geri
Both sides	2 × Kekomi

* The same defence must no be repeated on the same side.

Kata
Bassai-Dai, plus one previous kata.

1st KYU - BROWN + RED BELT

Command	
	Sanbon-tzuki
Turn	Sanbon-tzuki/Mae-geri/Sanbon-tzuki × 5
Forward + Back	Age-uke/Mae-geri/Gyaku-tzuki/Gedan-barai × 5
Forward + Back	Ude-uke/Empi/Uraken/Gyaku-tzuki/ Gedan-barai × 5
Forward + Back	Uchi-uke (Kokutsu-dachi)/Kizami-tzuki/ Gyaku-tzuki/Gedan-barai × 5
Forward + Back	Shutō-uke/Mawashi-geri (Front leg)/Nukite × 5
Turn	Mae-geri/Mawashi-geri/Uraken/ Gyaku-tzuki/Gedan-barai × 5 Mae-geri/Kekomi/Shutō-uchi/ Gyaku-tzuki/Gedan-barai × 5
Turn	Mae-geri/Kekomi/Shutō-uchi/ Gyaku-tzuki/Gedan-barai × 5
Both sides	Keage (Kiba-dachi)/Gyaku-tzuki (Zenkutsu-dachi)/Gedan-barai (Kiba-dachi) × 5 Ushiro-geri/Uraken/Gyaku-tzuki × 5
Turn	Ushiro-geri/Uraken/Gyaku-tzuki × 5 Kekomi (front leg)/Mae-geri (back leg) and step forward × 5
Turn	Kekomi (front leg)/Mae-geri (back leg) and step forward × 5
Both sides	Face the front; Mae-geri/Kekomi, with the same leg × 5
Both sides	Face the front; Mae-geri/Mawashi-geri, with the same leg × 5
Both sides	Face the front; Mae-geri/Kekomi/Ushiro-geri, with the same leg × 5

	Jiyu-Ippon Kumite
Both sides	2 × Jōdan
Both sides	2 × Chūdan
Both sides	2 × Mae-geri
Both sides	2 × Kekomi
Both sides	2 × Mawashi-geri

	and Kihon-Ippon Kumite*
Both sides	2 × Jōdan
Both sides	2 × Chūdan
Both sides	2 × Mae-geri
Both sides	2 × Kekomi
Both sides	2 × Mawashi-geri

* The same defence must not be repeated on the same side.

Kata. A choice of the one of the following: Kanku-Dai, Empi, Jihon, Jitte, Jiin, plus one previous kata

SHODAN

All kihon and combination techniques are performed from the free style position

Command	
	Kizami-tzuki/Mae-geri/Sanbon-tzuki × 5
Turn	Kizami-tzuki/Mae-geri/Sanbon-tzuki × 5
Forward + Back	Age-uke/Mae-geri/Gyaku-tzuki/Gedan-barai × 5
Forward + Back	Ude-uke/Empi/Uraken/Gyaku-tzuki/Gedan-barai × 5
Forward + Back	Uchi-uke (ko-kutsu-dachi)/Kizami-tzuki/ Gyaku-tzuki/Gedan-barai × 5
Forward + Back	Shutō-uke/Mawashi-geri (Front leg)/Nukite × 5
	Mae-geri/Mawashi-geri/Uraken/ Gyaku-tzuki/Gedan-barai × 5
Turn	Mae-geri/Mawashi-geri/Uraken/ Gyaku-tzuki/Gedan-barai × 5
	Mae-geri/Kekomi/Shutō-uchi/ Gyaku-tzuki/Gedan-barai × 5
Turn	Mae-geri/Kekomi/Shutō-uchi/ Gyaku-tzuki/Gedan-barai × 5
	Step back, Age-uke/Mawashi-geri (back leg)/Uraken/Oi-tzuki × 5
Turn	Step back, Age-uke/Mawashi-geri (back leg)/Uraken/Oi-tzuki × 5
	Mawashi-geri (front leg)/Ushiro-geri/ Uraken/Gyaku-tzuki × 5
Turn	Mawashi-geri (front left)/Ushiro-geri/ Uraken/Gyaku-tzuki × 5
	Kekomi (front leg)/Step forward, Mae-geri/Oi-tzuki/Gyaku-tzuki × 5
Turn	Kekomi (Front leg)/Step forward, Mae-geri/Oi-tzuki/Gyaku-tzuki × 5
	Keage/Kekomi, on the same leg stepping over × 5
Turn	Keage/Kekomi, on the same leg stepping over × 5
Both sides	Face the front, Mae-geri/Kekomi/ Ushiro-geri (with the same leg)

269

	Jiyu-Ippon Kumite *
Both sides	2 × Jōdan
Both sides	2 × Chūdan
Both sides	2 × Mae-geri
Both sides	2 × Kekomi
Both sides	2 × Mawashi-geri

	and *Kihon-Ippon Kumite* *
Both sides	2 × Jōdan
Both sides	2 × Chūdan
Both sides	2 × Mae-geri
Both sides	2 × Kekomi
Both sides	2 × Mawashi-geri

* The same defence must not be repeated on the same side.

Free style with two consecutive people
Kata. A choice of one of the following: Kanku-Dai, Empi, Jion, Jitte, Jiin, Gankaku, Hungetsu, plus one previous kata
Oral exam. On Karate-Do, including Japanese terminology. Interview to assess student's character.

NIDAN

Basics are the same as for Shodan with the addition of:

Kekomi (front leg)/Ushiro-geri/Shutō-uchi/Gyaku-tzuki
On the same leg; Mae-geri/Kekomi/Ushiro-geri/Mawashi-geri, and return to the starting position

Kumite consists of: OKURI Jiyu-Ippon (ONE SIDE ONLY)

1 × Jōdan
1 × Chūdan
1 × Mae-geri
1 × Kekomi
1 × Mawashi-geri
1 × Ushiro-geri

Free style with three consecutive people
Tokui Kata plus one previous kata
Oral exam as in Shodan

SANDAN

Demonstration of all basic techniques against a stationary target

Free style against five consecutive Dan grades
Tokui kata, plus interpretation and a kata of the Examiner's choice
Oral exam as in Nidan

IN CONCLUSION

After reading this book, for whatever it is worth, my sincere wish is that it will have contributed in some measure to your knowledge of Shotokan Karate and encouraged you to continue with the study of Karate-Do.

As a teacher of the art for many years now, I have seen a great number of people come, but alas – a great number of people go. Losing students is terribly disappointing, especially when considering the tremendous potential many of them appear to have.

First to go is the "undesirable", thankfully eliminating himself, closely followed by many of the "Instant Kickers". Those who have a natural aptitude for the physical accomplishments of Karate but quite early on, find it "All too easy" – and give up, without really having ever TRIED. Ultimately, that Western adage would seem to apply – "You can lead a horse to water..."

So who are the people who remain to become the teachers and masters of tomorrow? The answer to that question is, apart from a handful of naturally talented people – ordinary folk!

The art of Karate holds a mystical appeal for many. Initially perhaps, the ability of a man to put his hand through a brick and later the thought of becoming invincible, repelling any attack by any number of assailants. For the average man to acquire this knowledge and become "extraordinary", is perhaps, in the first instance an enthralling notion and an opportunity too good to miss. Of course, after several months of serious training the student realises he may never become a "Superman" and quite probably doesn't want to either. For the idea will be dawning, that the continued practise of basic fundamentals is having an effect on the way he sees, feels and behaves towards other people and at this point, he has begun his journey, along "The Way".

The physical movements of punching, kicking, striking and blocking performed repeatedly, are but a vehicle needed to transport the traveller along "The Way" to his appointed destination. The journey is a gradual one and cannot be undergone in a few months. There is no substitute for time – and that is what it takes.

Karate has been described as a "Moving Zen" and I personally believe it is akin to religion. It is about helping people, doing someone a good turn – not a bad one and above all humility. How clear are the words of "The Dojo Kun", if we can only live up to them.

Unfortunately, we are human, therefore imperfect, but the fact remains – it's not THE STYLE that is important but the way in which THE MAN conducts himself and sets an example for others to follow.

Karate-Do, practised sincerely, will build confidence, promote fitness, improve fighting ability and enhance longevity of life but these are small measure compared to the "Real" benefits awaiting you.

Left: Karate-Dō flourishing – in the English countryside

GLOSSARY

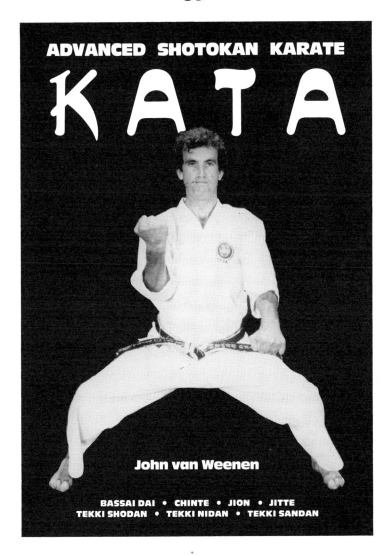

ADVANCED SHOTOKAN KARATE KATA BOOKS

The most comprehensive series of Shotokan Karate Kata Books yet produced.

IN THREE VOLUMES

Paul Hooley and Associates are proud to be associated with John van Weenen's expert works on Shotokan Karate Katas. The author together with leading photographer, Trevor Yorke, have combined to produce a series of books that make an outstanding contribution to the Art of Shotokan Karate.

VOLUME ONE AVAILABLE NOW	VOLUME TWO FORTHCOMING	VOLUME THREE PUBLICATIONS
1. **Bassai Dai**	8. **Wankan**	15. **Kanku-Sho**
2. **Chinte**	9. **Ji'in**	16. **Enpi**
3. **Jion**	10. **Sochin**	17. **Unsu**
4. **Jitte**	11. **Kanku-Dai**	18. **Seienchin**
5. **Tekki Shodan**	12. **Gankaku**	19. **Hangetsu**
6. **Tekki Nidan**	13. **Meikyo**	20. **Nijushiho**
7. **Tekki Sandan**	14. **Bassai-Sho**	21. **Gojushiho-Dai**
		22. **Gojushiho-Sho**

Each volume measuring 11¾ in. × 8¼ in. (international A4 size) with its glossy full colour laminated cover, contains a complete breakdown of the Kata, movement by movement. Volume one alone has 195 action packed pages containing over 1,375 photographs.

Three sets of photographs have been used. The first shows the main movements of the Kata, the second how to move from one movement to the next, depicting all the intermediate moves, which often cause tremendous confusion. The third set illustrates the Kata's practical applications, explaining virtually every movement many of which, appear for the first time in print.

Adequate text about each movement provides information on stance, body shifting, speed, breathing and direction. The latter utilising John van Weenen's revolutionary "compass system" which explains with the utmost simplicity the direction to move in.

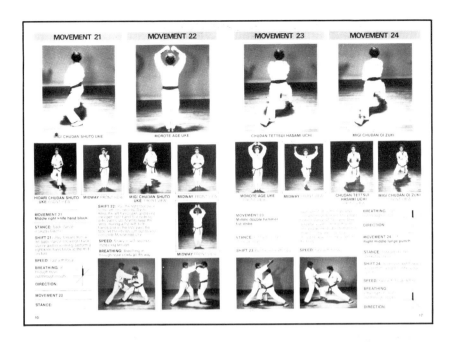

A typical spread of pages from one of the books

Each book contains a brief history of Karate and each individual Kata, together with a short explanation of the ten considerations of Yoi No Kisin, Inyo, Chikara No Kyojaku, Waza No Kankyo, Tai No Shinshuku, Kokyu, Tyakugan, Kiai, Keitai No Hoji and Zanshin, essential for its correct performance.

To have your name added to our mailing list, and to receive early notification of forthcoming publications, please write to:
Giko Ltd
537 Stratford Road, Sparkhill, Birmingham B11 4LP.
Tel: 021-773 9247/8.

Who said "Women are the weaker sex?" A light hearted moment during a recent ladies Karate and self defence course.